THE
GOLDEN CIRCLE

THE
GOLDEN CIRCLE

A Book of Months

By Hal Borland Paintings by Anne Ophelia Dowden

THOMAS Y. CROWELL COMPANY NEW YORK

Library of Congress Cataloging in Publication Data
Borland, Hal Glen   The golden circle.
SUMMARY: Text and paintings provide panoramic and
miniature views of the natural world month-by-month.
1. Seasons—Juv. lit. 2. Natural history—
United States—Juv. lit. [1. Seasons.
2. Natural history] I. Dowden, Anne Ophelia Todd
II. Title. QH81.B7415   500.9   77-23560   ISBN 0-690-03803-8

1   2   3   4   5   6   7   8   9   10

For Barbara Borland and Ray Dowden,
who share the love and respect for the
natural world that are so important
to the author and the artist

Contents

THE
GOLDEN CIRCLE

The Close View
and the Far Horizon

This is a book about the world around us, the natural world of grass and trees and flowers and vines, of brooks and ponds and oozing bogs, of birds and butterflies and frogs and fiddling crickets. It is about sunrise and the full moon and snowflakes and autumn leaves. It is words and pictures to help the reader to see and recognize these aspects and details of the natural world.

In writing the text, the author has taken the big, panoramic view, reaching out in all directions to help the reader feel and hear and see what nature is doing and what the natural world looks like month by month. In creating the pictures, however, the artist has chosen the more intimate view, the miniature, one might say, looking more closely at sources and beginnings. We believe that the two combined present a better picture than either could alone. The casual observer who sees only high hills, tall trees and saucer-size sunflowers may be reminded that there are also

1

knolls, shrubs and such blossoms as violets and anemones. And the admirer of minutiae may become aware that pasture thistles and great mulleins and wild parsnips grow only a few steps from the tiny maiden pink.

That is one reason this book about the year, month by month, asks on one page that you look at the miniatures and on the next page tells you how beautiful are the distant hilltops at dusk.

Much of the text deals with nature out beyond the urban centers. This is no mere whim on my part, though I live on a farm in an area of wooded hills and cultivated valleys. The cities of this country really occupy only about 5 percent of its total area. That leaves 95 percent of it rural. The natural world is never very far away, no matter where you may live.

But any city will have places where nature persists or is preserved and encouraged, parks and other areas of grass and trees and some kind of natural growth. Flowers will bloom there, and leaves will change color in autumn. Because cities are warmer than the open countryside, the timing will be different, but the sequence will be the same. Seeds sprout, grow, put out leaves and buds, come to blossom and make seeds for another year, no matter where they grow. The artist found some of her subjects in New York City, in fact, though most came from rural New Jersey, New Hampshire and other countrysides.

One other note about the pictures. What you see here, you can find in its natural setting, and the same size as the pictures show. That is one reason there are no big, spectacular autumn leaves of the maple or the oak or the beech trees. Instead, there are the miniature leaves of blueberries, spireas, chokeberries, honeysuckles, dainty and vividly colored but not so big that one or two leaves cover the page.

2

So, one way and another, Anne Ophelia Dowden and I have here presented aspects of the natural world that we hope will help the reader to see and understand. This is our environment, the place we live and have our being. It is ours to cherish and protect. Our purpose is to help others to know and cherish it.

H.B., 1977

JANUARY

The first day of the first month of a new year is something like Genesis—anything is possible. Possible, but perhaps not probable. That, after all, is as much as anyone should ask of life, the possibilities. From there on it is largely up to us. To us, and to circumstances. Time and again we arrive at the point of decision, the fork in the road and a choice to be made. We make the choice and go on; but the outcome has been influenced by circumstances, perhaps by chance. Our lives are dominated by choice and circumstance.

But there are constantly recurring times of new beginnings, as today when all things, as I was saying, are possible. Here is another unused span of that indeterminate interval between birth and death, another series of days, good, bad, ordinary, extraordinary, 365 days. Here is the first page of a brand-new calendar. Here is January.

Plants from the edge of a pasture:
Evening primrose, St. John's wort, Dewberry, Aster

Now comes the long, slow haul up the cold slope toward spring and April. The cold days and the long nights are ours, the best and the worst of winter. Long nights and early evenings, fireside evenings for long thoughts and simple comforts. Star nights, when the old patterns in the sky gleam with a promise of the nearest certainty, the most enduring continuity, visible from any window or any snowy road. Late dawns, when the gray world comes alive after darkness and chill that seemed so deep they might last forever. High noon, with the sun so far off to the south that only the faith of generations can believe it will be overhead again, come June.

January, which drives man in upon himself and tests his mettle.

January is the coldest month, the darkest and sometimes the snowiest. In my part of the world this is the time when the rocks have lost the last of their autumn warmth and the earth itself heaves with deep-biting frost. Now the seep among the stones becomes the ice lever that pries ridges apart. Now the ice shoulders the river valleys and splits the granite ledges and loosens the soil in the meadow. This is the time of inexorable forces working silently all around us.

But the ice will pass, with the passing of the long nights. Streams will flow free again, and rocks will lie warm in the sun. Birds will sing and trees will burst bud and put forth leaves once more. By January's end the daylight will be three-quarters of an hour longer than it is at the beginning. The slope lessens as we climb from winter's depth. It always has. We cannot believe it will fail to now.

January was named for one of the principal Roman gods, Janus, the god of beginnings and the custodian of the universe.

6

The first hour of the day, the first day of the month, the first month of the year, all were sacred to him. But his chief function was as guardian of gates and doorways. He was represented as a two-faced god whose head had a face at the back as well as the front, symbolic of his ability to face both past and future at the same time.

A new year begins, we say. But the latent bud on the branch doesn't stir, the blossom in the bulb sleeps undisturbed in the frozen ground. The woodchuck's hibernating pulse doesn't quicken one beat, and the deer in the thicket is just as hungry as he was yesterday. Man is the only animal to whom this new year is important.

Hemlock

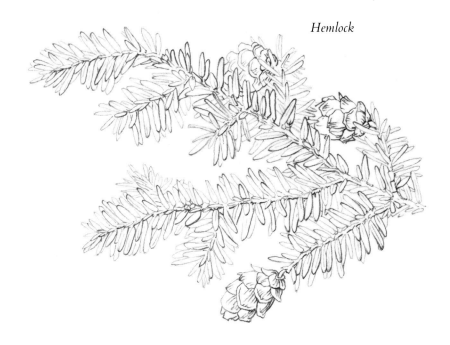

Before the month is out you will hear the blue jays calling, a cheerful, musical two-note call quite unlike the raucous jeer they have been uttering all winter. Tree sparrows will begin to sing. Their songs are nothing like the music of song sparrows, but they are sweet, high-pitched and surprising after having heard nothing from them but a twitter for so long. Even the nuthatches will change their inflection. They will still *yark-yark*, but happily instead of querulously.

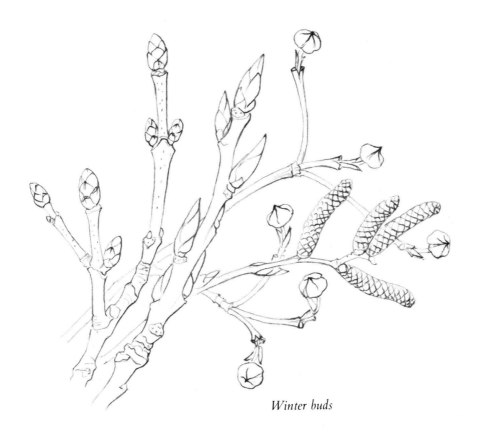

Winter buds

MARCH

March was named for the Roman god Mars. Some explain this in terms of the warring weather systems that dominate March weather. That reference, of course, is to Mars as the god of war. But in early Roman times Mars was the god of agriculture, of growing plants, and this identity may have been the original significance of the month's name. The Saxons, however, called it Lenet-monat, or length-month, because this is when daylight begins to lengthen beyond darkness. That Saxon name, incidentally, was the origin of the term Lent.

In England March usually is spring, with English daisies coming to blossom, spring bulbs in flower, birds starting to sing, and with mild weather the rule. Here in America March is quite another matter, but for a long time the literary poets of this country tried to persuade their countrymen that March was as mild and friendly here as in England. What they were doing, of

Plants from a country roadside:
Periwinkle, Coltsfoot

13

course, was writing paeans to spring based on English poems instead of venturing outdoors or even looking out their own windows and writing about what actually was there. It wasn't until Thoreau's day that we began to have poetry about the American spring as it emerges from the American soil. Not the best poetry, let's admit, but with the breath of our own outdoors in it.

Our March is pussy willows, at latest by midmonth. It is redwing blackbirds and migrant robins. It usually is spring peepers. It is colt's foot on sunny, gravelly slopes, false dandelion to the casual passerby. It is February's crocuses multiplied a hundredfold. It is the deep purplish blue of vinca, or periwinkle, on steep banks where wise gardeners planted it. All this, and March is snow and ice and thaw and mud and wind and more snow and cold rain. It often floods the lowlands, sometimes the major river valleys. March is maple sap flowing, and hence the year's first crop—maple sugar and maple syrup. And March brings the vernal equinox.

March really is a bit of everything and, in weather terms, is as whimsical as the proverbial hare. The reason is that the earth is beginning to warm up after three months in cold storage. This sets new air currents in motion. Warm air rises, cold air rushes in, is warmed and also rises, and more cold air takes its place. Hence, March is windy and can be stormy. It starts with February's leftovers, which can be a snowstorm or a late February thaw. Whichever it is, it probably will not last long.

On the old rural calendars this was a time for sulphur and molasses to tone up the blood. Winter, it was said, thickened the blood. Some said just the opposite, that it thinned the blood. In either case, sulphur and molasses brought the blood back to a normal consistency. If it was an early spring, this dosing was followed by a big helping of dandelion greens. If you survived that, you got stewed rhubarb in April. The only way to escape was to look and act far more healthy than you felt. Few people succeeded. But the threat of sulphur and molasses, or dandelions, or rhubarb did much to drive the winter lethargy out of one's bones.

When spring peepers call before March ends, the whole year seems to be in proper order, the rhythm as it should be. The peepers are primitive and ancient, and spring is very old and very simple.

Spring peepers

APRIL

April is spring, but spring isn't all lilacs and apple blossoms, orioles and scarlet tanagers. The spring most of us live with has frosty mornings and usually a light snowfall in April. True, the migrant robins have returned, the peepers have been out and calling for a few days, bees have been busy at the crocuses. And if you look among the leaf litter at the edge of the woods you will find hepatica with its pale lavender or white blossoms. Look down along the brook and see trout lilies with golden-yellow flowers and mottled twin leaves, true lilies though sometimes called dog-tooth violets. Look on any rural hillside and watch the tiny white wood anemones, wind flowers, literally, that nod in the slightest breeze. But April is a beginning, not an achievement. One thinks ahead now, to May and June.

We have passed the equinox and to some extent that has altered the weather systems. The earth has begun to shed its winter chill. A good deal of the frost is out of the ground. But no equinox ever yet has sprouted a radish seed. That takes sunlight and warm rain and soil warm enough to melt a snowflake. That calls for spring as a reality, not a date on a calendar. Spring is essentially earthy. You can listen a long time and not hear a robin say "Equinox."

Man did not invent April or set spring's alarm clock. All man can do about spring is guess when it will come and cooperate with it when it arrives. That way we manage to grow corn and oats and lettuce and green beans and maintain rather a precarious foothold here. We have created the fiction that man owns and controls the earth, and what we have done to the earth is rapacious beyond belief. But every spring you can see April denying the human boast of omnipotence. Nobody has yet taken the icy nip out of an April frost. Nobody has yet persuaded the sun to rise ten minutes early or delay its setting by one tick of the clock. Nobody has halted the greening of grass or forbidden the shadbush to come to snowy blossom by law or edict. We can wall ourselves away from sky, earth and weather in city apartment or office, but April will summon spring to the city and set pulses throbbing with vernal urgencies.

The April the countryfolk know is beyond the reach of court or legislature. It starts with early saxifrage like deep frost on the ledges, with hepatica in bloom nearby, with peepers shrilling, with redwing blackbirds *kareeing*, with robins saluting the sunrise. By the second week the flickers have come back and towhees are making the leaves fly in the litter of last fall's discard. Woodpeckers are rapping out summonses and announcements on dead trees. Song sparrows and whitethroats are singing loudly, and cardinals and orioles are on hand for the morning chorus.

18

By the time the maples bloom the warblers have begun to come through on their way north and mid-April is past. Violets make the brookside purple. Jack-in-the-pulpit opens its spathe and leaves. Bloodroot opens its big white waxen blossoms beside old stone walls, and fern fiddleheads are in sight. Wild columbine is in bud. Frogs emerge and trill, and peepers lay their eggs in the frigid bog water.

April leads to May, to spring in full flower.

Maple flowers

MAY

May is so many good things it is hard to choose, so take them all and enjoy them. But give us apple blossoms and lilacs, and a good many of us will be content. Especially if you add violets.

Apple orchards are specially beautiful in May, but in lower New England there are old apple trees on remote hillsides that make one think of Johnny Appleseed. His name really was John Chapman and he was born in Massachusetts, but he spent much of his life wandering through what then was the Ohio Country and mostly Indian land, planting apple trees as he went. The beauty of his wild orchards along the streams of the American Midlands in any May must have been breathtaking for the old wanderer. Primitive Christian that he was, Johnny must have exclaimed many times at the beauty of God's work and the bounty of His benevolent hand.

Plants from the edge of a meadow:
Cinquefoil, Violet

One gets something of the same feeling when one finds gnarled old apple trees in bloom on remote hillsides here in lower New England. There usually are only two or three left, and unless there is a cellar hole nearby it is hard to tell whether some long-forgotten settler planted them or they were wildlings. But they are very old, broken-limbed, maimed by winter storms, and still lifting blossom-laden boughs like offerings to the sun. All around them are seedlings, shoots sprung from windfall seeds and surviving only thanks to oversight by deer and rabbits. The air now is loud with their company of bees and faintly spiced with the fragrance of their blossoms.

On another hillside is an old lilac bush beside a shallow, overgrown hollow that unmistakably once was the cellar of an early settler's home. Faithfully it comes to bloom about the time the apple trees are in blossom. And all around are violets and creeping cinquefoil, the five-leaf false strawberry with yellow blossoms, reminders of some woman's hunger for beauty beside her door.

Bloodroot still stands white along gray stone walls. Jack-in-the-pulpit is in full bloom, and trillium, handsome to look at, fetid to smell. The brilliant yellow of marsh marigold has faded. Columbines are in full bloom by midmonth.

Brooks still run bankful, and the pond—it becomes a minor swamp in August—is lapping at its own high-water mark, though April's rains are past. May, initially at least, is all sunshine and growth.

And there is the profundity of May. The notion persists that anything with a depth of meaning must be hard to understand, must be written in an obscure language. Yet here is May, a time of fundamental and miraculous matters, all of them spread before us flagrantly demanding attention. Its language is as simple as a new maple leaf or a buttercup blossom.

Here is the fundamental of life, the whole process of germination and growth. Here is flowering and fertility and life preparing its own renewal. Here are sunlight and water being turned into food by photosynthesis, an even more profound process than atomic fusion, and it goes on in every blade of grass, every tree leaf, no more secret than sunlight. Here is abundance, growth and beneficence, so much that the world seems hard put to contain it all. It constantly spills over.

Here is May.

Honeybees and apple blossoms

JUNE

June comes with its own tranquillity, predictable as sunrise, reassuring as dusk. The grass grows toward maturity, ready for the haymakers. Trees cast their shade as they have since the hills were young. On those hills the most dwarfed of the dogwoods, the one commonly called bunchberry, opens its cluster of tiny blossoms in the center of the four large white petal-like bracts, flowers that will be vivid scarlet berries before the end of August. Wild strawberries ripen, honey-sweet, as they ripened long before white men knew there was an America. Brooks make their way to rivers and rivers flow to the sea as they have since water first ran downhill. There is a certainty, an undiminished truth, in sunlight and rain and the fertility of the seed.

Nature has no object lessons, but June and summer bring the undeniable truth of growth and continuity. Every summer since the earth achieved the first green leaf has been another link in the

Plants from the edge of a woods:
Wild strawberry, Bunchberry, Veronica

chain of verity that is there for understanding. Every field, every meadow, every roadside now is rich with the sustaining truth of abundance, evidence that the earth is essentially a hospitable place for life, no matter what follies man may commit. June is a season for repairing the human perspective; for admitting, however privately, that there are forces and rhythms that transcend man's arrogance and his transient plans.

June is March and April brought to the enduring truth of summer. It is the whole sustaining principle of life and growth, from seed to stem to leaf, from blossom to seed again. That is the eternal rhythm.

By the sign we call the solstice the first three weeks of June are still spring. But the solstice is no more than one point on a circle, that moment when the earth begins to swing back on its trunnions and the hours of daylight start their creeping abbreviation once more. The solstice passes, and we say it is summer, and there is no pause in the bee drone over the clover field, no pause in the growth of the green stalks in the cornfield.

Taken literally, solstice means that the sun stands still. That is an illusion, for there is no standing still any place, any time. The earth turns, the year turns, sunrise and sunset change, day by day by day. Nor does man stand still, nor man's affairs. Change is the only constant, even in leisurely June. Trees grow, corn grows tall, and man must grow and ripen with them, even as the sun goes through its cycle. To plant, to harvest, to learn, to understand— that is the law of time. The solstice is the year's meridian, not its resting place.

To stop time, to make the sun stand still, to have June for twice its actual span—that has been the dream of many dreamers. To decide and act, and to have the chance to redecide and act anew on the same problem. But no problem is ever the same twice, nor is any day exactly like another. The seed sprouts, grows, and there is a harvest. We move on, day to day, solstice to equinox, webbed in time.

June and fireflies, June and roses, June and the fledgling on the wing. June and its incredible greenness, its meadow-frost of daisies, its hoped-for happiness, its longed-for beauty, its dreams that could come true five minutes from now. And overhead, underfoot, all around is the remembering, the knowing, the very being of June, the partaking and the foreverness, the sweet foreverness of June.

Wild rose

JULY

By July it is so summery that it is easy to forget spring. We are surrounded by so much evidence of achievement that what went into it, like the details of so many beginnings, is a part of some dim yesterday. It seems impossible that today's bee hum and harvest-fly buzz, corn-pollen scent, ripe-oat gold and new hay in the barns were egg and seed and awakening root only a few months ago. July seems so complete it might have been here for years and so enduring it might last for another decade.

Midsummer brings this dual sense of time, particularly in the country. There is the foreverness, this almost droning completion, and there is the day-to-day urgency and the sense of time passing swiftly. Days are long and full. To the countryfolk they are a kind of delayed payment for the short days of abbreviated demand that were theirs in January. Now they buy their winter leisure. Yet they live in the midst of a world that is almost through with its hurrying, has passed its springtime urgency; a world where grass grows silently and high cumulus clouds drift lazily across the sky; where fireflies sparkle the night, luna moths fray their fragile wings at screened windows and whippoorwills call monotonously.

Spring is pressure building up to the green explosion of May, and May itself such energetic haste that it seems impossible that its major sounds are bird songs. The urgencies carry over into June before they begin to ease toward the fulfillment of July. By now we are almost as sated as the noontime bumblebee, accepting this green world as the norm, forgetting April, forgetting unforgettable winter.

But we can live with summer. We don't have to wall and woollen ourselves from it. We can even feel we are partners in its achievements, albeit definitely junior partners. If we get too arrogant a July thunderstorm claps our ears or a tornado makes us think twice about the degree of our omnipotence. Summer supplies its own correctives. But if we are willing to live with it, not try to dictate to it, we make out surprisingly well. The hours are long and the sweat comes easily; but it always has been difficult to build anything enduring, including freedom, without a good deal of hard work, and nobody has yet invented a better lubricant for the gears of human achievement than sweat.

The season actually begins to lean toward autumn in July, though we always are reluctant to admit it. Once we have passed the solstice we are on the long incline that leads to October and the falling leaf. Daylight begins to shorten. The sun, as we say, already is edging southward again. Fledglings are on the wing. Brooks languish into midsummer slack and rivers are tepid and lazy.

Go to the country and you will see highways edged with bird's-foot trefoil, its buttery yellow little flowers twice as yellow with the orange splashes of black-eyed Susans just beyond. Rabbit-foot clover makes low hedges along side roads, with the froth of Queen Anne's lace, the wild carrot, edging the meadows. Milkweed comes to bloom with a tuberose scent for the evening air. The wood thrush sings its contralto song in the twilight and fireflies freckle the night. The jubilance of June has settled into the stridulated insistence of midsummer's insects. July possesses the land.

Swallowtail butterfly and milkweed

AUGUST

Now come those hot, humid August days of summer at its very peak. Now, according to old superstitions, dogs go mad, snakes bite without provocation, and there is miasma in the air over the lowlands. All of which has just enough truth to keep the superstitions alive. Dogs sometimes are rabid in August, and so are skunks, foxes and other animals; they are rabid in other months too, however. Snakes shed their skins now and, both blind and testy when moulting, strike at anything that disturbs them. Ponds are stagnant, but it is their insect swarms, not their vapors, that are poisonous—mosquitoes abound.

Inheriting our traditions from the Romans, we call the season dog days; the old Roman soothsayers blamed such troubles on the Dog Star. Had we inherited from the Egyptians, our late summer tradition would dictate a time of thanksgiving now, for this was the time when the Nile flooded and gave Egypt's

Plants from a hemlock woods: 33
Indian pipe, Bunchberry

farmland its annual renewal of fertility. The Egyptians celebrated a time the Romans feared.

For us today, August brings the tang of corn pollen in the air, the taste of roasting ears at the table. It brings a display of goldenrod along the fencerows, which always makes the season seem later than it is; goldenrod is a warning that daisies and black-eyed Susans are fading and asters soon will possess the roadsides. August brings ripe tomatoes, and the big green tomato worm that will pupate and emerge on wings as a beautiful sphinx moth. It brings another cutting of hay to the loft, another picking of green beans to the freezer.

August brings Bouncing Bet to blossom at the roadside, a pink brought here from Europe by early settlers both as a garden flower and as a root to suds the water to wash milady's hair. It brings sour dock and smartweed to seed that proves their kinship to buckwheat. Before August ends, ragweed comes to inconspicuous blossom and poisons the air for allergic people with its pollen.

In damp, shaded woodland the ghost flowers we know as Indian pipe come to bloom, grayish-white with a hint of pink on stem, leaf and blossom. Parasites, they live on decaying vegetation. Pick one for an indoor vase and it soon withers and turns black in your hand.

Early apples ripen. Katydids scratch the night, warning of frost in six more weeks. Anglers have scant luck because the fish are sated in waters that now are a rich soup of larval life. Green acorns hang on the oaks, resiny green cones on pine and spruce. Chokeberries ripen, and dark-juiced elderberries.

Where red-osier stems blushed in April, now is a wealth of lead-gray berries, and on their silky cornel cousins is a ripening harvest of dull blue fruit. The highbush cranberry, which is no cranberry at all but a viburnum, shows yellow on its berries, then orange. Before frost they will be cranberry red and cranberry tart.

August is joe-pye weed coming to blossom, and ironweed, and vervain in low, wet places. It is cattails holding high their fat new thumbs. It is the great mullein in leisurely bloom, wild snapdragon in butter-and-eggs display, virgin's bower turning into bristly old man's beard.

It is a laggard sun, earlier to bed, later to rise. August is summer sliding down that long slope into autumn.

Red eft

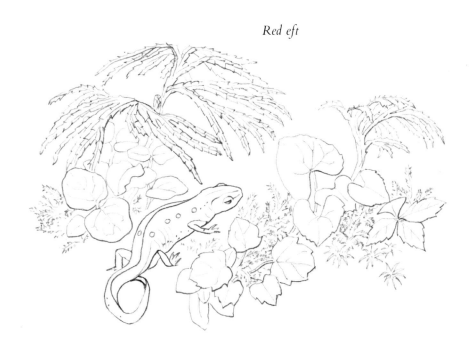

SEPTEMBER

September is both more than a month and less, for it is almost a season in itself. It is flickers in restless flocks, readying for migration. It is goldfinches in a glistening cloud of thistledown. It is the gleam of goldenrod and the white and lavender and purple of fencerow asters, with the bright spangle of partridgeberries beginning to ripen.

September is fog over the river valleys at dawn and the creep of early scarlet among the maples in the swamp. It is sumac in war paint. It is bronze of hillside grass gone to seed. It is walnuts ripening and squirrels busy among the hickories. It is late phlox like a flame in the garden, and zinnias in bold color, and chrysanthemums budding. It is a last gallant flaunt of portulaca and petunias defying time and early frost.

The owl has hooted in the evening darkness. The voice of autumn has echoed across the valley. There is no mistaking it, for although the green world is still green it has the gleam of dogwood berries, the smell of windfall apples in the orchard and the wine tang in the vineyard. You can close your eyes and know what is happening.

Ripeness is fulfillment, and it comes not at the peak of summer. It comes when the season begins to ease down the long hill toward winter and ice, when the days shorten and the stars of night begin to gleam in longer darkness. Ripeness is a summation of long, hot days and simmering sun and warm rain and the flash of lightning across the summer sky. It is the beauty of the blossom brought to the succulence of the fruit, the soft green of the new stem toughened to the firm fiber of the reaching twig, the winged seed of the maple now rooted in the grass and finding sustenance in the soil.

The change is more than a matter of sunlight and day length, for there is a rhythm in all growing things, a rest and a resurgence. The seasons belong to that rhythm, as do the day and the night. So do the apple, the goldenrod, the asters. So do the mushrooms and most of the fungi, but with a difference. An autumn rain, a few hot September days, and mushrooms will appear overnight in woodland shade or on grassy, sunlit dooryards, wherever their spores lay waiting. They grow as if by magic, almost as you watch, some of them beautiful as exotic flowers, and ripen spores and shrink and are gone in a few days, in less time than the reddening of a sumac leaf.

There is color in the woods, but it still is tentative. A few maples show red, one branch on a big tree, a small seedling all in color. The start. Actually, the brightest color in the woods just now is that of the woodbine, or Virginia creeper.

You see Virginia creeper on a tall, dead elm, and the scarlet leaves make that old tree a pillar of fire. You see poison ivy on another dead elm, and it, too, is beautiful—from a distance. The ivy leaves are three-part, remember, and have an oily look, and the vine has lead-gray berries. Virginia creeper's fruit is like miniature wild grapes, purple.

As the chill of September nights reaches over into the daylight hours there is a quickening of the human pulse. There is new vigor in the air. But in the insect world the fires burn low. The bugs and the beetles are nearing the end of their time. We approach deep frost and the long, deep quiet until another spring, a quiet so intense you can hear a snowflake falling in the night.

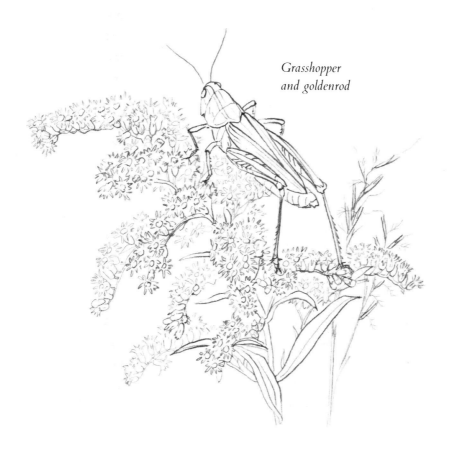

*Grasshopper
and goldenrod*

OCTOBER

October is ripeness, in the fields, on the trees, the bushes, the vines. The acorn and the wild grape achieve their purpose, to the satisfaction of the squirrel and the possum and to the propagation of their own species. All the viburnums are bright with berries, as they were white with blossoms and loud with bees only a few months ago. The milkweed pods are ready to burst and strew the autumn wind with shimmer. The tang of windfalls scents the autumn air where white apple blossoms made May a delight to the eye.

Here in my own hills October is the time of asters, an astonishing and most satisfying display of those particular composite flowers whose hardiest members will outlast the month itself. I know a place where a back road cuts through a steep hill and creates banks too steep to mow. The sun lingers late and the chill winds blow right over it. Wildflowers thrive on those banks as in few other places I know, early spring, midsummer and late fall. Now that steeply banked roadside is an almost solid mass of asters, as magnificent a show as anyone could ask, white to purple and all the shades of lavender and blue, small as a fingernail, big as a silver dollar. I have counted fifteen species there without half trying. October is Aster Month.

October also is Maple Month. Now the maples assert themselves, particularly here in the Northeast. They paint whole landscapes red and gold and all the tones, tints and shades between. They are the particular glory of our woodlands. The sugar maples—hard maples, rock maples, whatever you choose to call them—in some areas turn so yellow they create their own sunshine on a cloudy day. In other places they turn orange and red. The red maples—or soft or swamp maples; again, choose your name—create those flaming valleys that look like rivers and lakes of live coals among the golden hills.

Even the lesser ones of the woodland, the shrubs and bushes, now assert their colorful selves. The various blueberries with leaves no bigger than a fingernail make hillside pools of deep red and purple. Chokeberries reflect their vanished fruit in their October leaves. The spireas are bright as new buttons. A cluster of scarlet berries marks the place where Jack stood in his pulpit three months ago.

But October is more than trees, more than bright berries and ripened nuts. It is the year's achievement, the summary of March melt and April warmth, of June's mellow moonlight and July's crackling thunderstorms. It is the sprout grown into the stalk, the bud become the blossom and the blossom the seed. It is the geese honking high and the call to far places, the hunter on the hill, the hound belling the night. It is the snug cabin, the soup kettle a-simmer, the woman singing a gladsome song.

42

October is a time of far and misty horizons that beckon, a time of crow-caw and jay-jeer, before the slash of sleet or the gentle fall of snow. It is frost creeping down from the hills on moccasin-quiet feet to dust the valleys with glitter, of wind skittering down the road in a scuffling of leaves, of owl hoot and fox bark in the moonlight. Stars twinkle again, in October, their summer glow polished to a gleam by the winds of autumn. October's full moon is the Hunter's Moon, almost as lasting as was the Harvest Moon of September.

Bumblebees and aster

NOVEMBER

November is berry-bright and firelight-gay, a glittering night, a crisp blue day, a whispering wind and a handful of determined fencerow asters. It is a lithe hemlock in a green lace party dress, and a clean-limbed gray birch laughing in the wind. It is apple cider with champagne beads of authority. It is a gray squirrel in the limber top of a hickory tree, graceful as the wind; it is a doe and her fawns munching windfall winesaps in the moonlit orchard. November is a handful of snowflakes flung over a Berkshire hilltop, and a woodchuck sniffing the wind and retreating to his den to sleep till April.

Our northern land begins to tuck itself in for the winter. Frost, wind and rain bring down the leaves and the season's coverlet starts to take shape in the woodland. It is still restless, the gusting wind rustling and shifting the leaves even in the hillside thickets, strewing them over the meadows, heaping them in the fence

Plants from a hedgerow:
Bittersweet, Witch hazel, St. John's wort,
Ground-cherry, Curly dock, Swamp milkweed

corners. Sometimes it seems that the leaves themselves are restless, reluctant to be earth-bound. After all, they are winged and they had an airy lifetime, and now they are free to ride each passing breeze. But the restlessness will pass. In a few more weeks they will settle down to blanket the earth, to dull the fang of frost for the wild seed and root and bulb.

November is the evening of the year, the bedtime of the green and flowering world. Now comes the time for sleep, for rest. The coverlet is being spread. Next should come the lullaby; but the lullaby singers have all gone south. The pines and the hemlocks will whisper good night instead.

The quiet comes and deepens, the winter quiet that waits on no arbitrary season of calendar or solstice. It is not only an aural quiet but a visual one, seen and felt as well as heard. Insects that buzzed and hummed and scratched are silenced now except an occasional fireside cricket. And the songbirds have gone south, leaving the countryside to the crows, the jays and the lesser birds that gossip among themselves but do little town crying and engage in no concerts.

The visual quiet is almost as complete. Maples stand in gray and brown nakedness, even the drift of their leaves dulled by early leaching of rain and frost. Oaks, their trunks black with the damp of morning mist, wear tatters of old, worn buckskin in their clinging leaves. The sumac is a lifting of gnarled, frost-blackened fingers toward the distant sun.

Insistently contrary, witch hazel comes to bloom with its tousle of bright yellow petals. Here and there you see the blush of wild rose haws or the warmth of orange berries on the bittersweet. Back in the woods is the occasional twinkle of partridgeberries. Milkweed floss drifts on the wind and the emptying pods are like

46

mother-of-pearl. But these are the gem stones and rare decorations which make the grays and browns and even the green of pine and hemlock seem even more quiet, more completely at rest. The stubborn simplicities of the earth are everywhere.

The urgencies have eased for another season. Only the wind hurries now. The cicada and the katydid have retreated to the silence of the egg. The frog has buried himself in the mud and the woodchuck sleeps only a few degrees this side of death. Soon even the rain will flake down and ice will pry at the fundamental rocks.

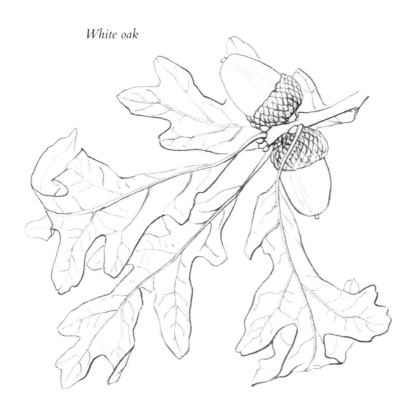

White oak

47

DECEMBER

December is a blizzard in Wyoming and a gale on the Lakes and the Berkshires frosted like a plate of cupcakes. It is bare trees and evergreens. It is rustling weed stems and a gleam of partridge-berry on the hillside, a cluster of checkerberries and winter-greens in the thin woodland. It is ground pine, older than the hills where it grows, and it is a seedling maple from two years ago clinging to one last scarlet leaf. It is a stiff-tailed young squirrel scrambling up an oak tree, and it is a mask-faced coon in the cornfield listening for the hounds. It is ice on the pond, lichen on the rock, a flock of chickadees at the dooryard feeder.

December is the first snow, usually. Snow that nourishes and protects the countryman's fields and pastures and even helps to seal and insulate his house and barns against the cruelest bite of winter. But in city and suburb snow has become a cold and slushy nuisance when it isn't a costly problem. To travelers everywhere

Plants from a pine forest:
Partridgeberry, Wintergreen, Club moss

snow is a blinding, slippery hazard to foot and wheel and wing.

Yet the snowflake itself is a thing of fragile, evanescent beauty. It is a delicate water crystal, one of the most transient of all natural forms, a wisp of mist that briefly acquired tangible shape. A snowfall can transform a woodland into a place of magic, a meadow into a shimmering wonderland. A snowdrift is the frozen grace of the wind, perfection in line and curve and form. Snow can temporarily restore the lost innocence to a scarred and naughty world of disillusionment and folly.

December nights are star nights, with winter-brilliant skies. When I walk the country road these evenings the whole universe accompanies me, for the earth is all open to the starlight, leaf fall complete. The stars lean so close that if I stood on tiptoe on the highest hill I might grasp at least one star in my tingling fingers.

It is an illusion, but the December stars seem twice as brilliant as those of June, for the sky is doubly clear. The mist is chilled out of it and the dust of summer has settled out of it, at last. An illusion, but a pleasant one on a brittle evening; the sun seems so far away that the stars should come closer. We should be able to glimpse eternity through those spark-holes in the blanket of the long night. And perhaps we do. Where else is such order, such an eternal pattern, as there is in those stars that light the December sky?

Now the year begins to sum up, in its own inconclusive way. In the continuity of time, winter overlaps the years and makes any summary incomplete; but there have been sprouting and leafing, there have been flowering and maturity, there have been harvest and the falling leaf. Now there is rest, quiet, a time of forces consolidated, which is as near to summary as any year affords.

50

Life is not all of a piece and never was. Life is change. Life is cause and life is effect, and there is no escape from that. Those who would put a price on things can say December is the price we pay for June. But even that distorts the impersonal cycle of time and life.

December, the winter solstice, the holy days of Christmas. Year's end, which is no end at all except on the calendar. Year builds upon year, even as the seasons follow, and year's end is only a pause, a time for a deep breath. Tomorrow rises in the east, all the tomorrows.

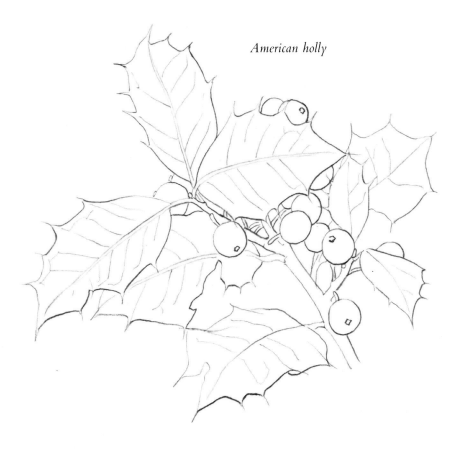

American holly

Names of Plants

JANUARY

Plants from the edge of a pasture:

Evening primrose—*Oenothera biennis*; St. John's wort—*Hypericum perforatum*; Dewberry—*Rubus* sp.; Aster—*Aster cordifolius*

FEBRUARY

Plants from a garden:

Winter aconite—*Eranthis hyemalis*; Crocus—*Crocus vernus, C. chrysanthus*; Snowdrop—*Galanthus nivalis*

MARCH

Plants from a country roadside:

Periwinkle—*Vinca minor*; Coltsfoot—*Tussilago farfara*

APRIL

Plants from an oak woods:

Hepatica—*Hepatica americana*; Trout lily—*Erythronium americanum*

MAY

Plants from the edge of a meadow:

Cinquefoil—*Potentilla simplex*; Violet—*Viola papilionacea*

JUNE
Plants from the edge of a woods:

Wild strawberry—*Fragaria virginiana*; Bunchberry—*Cornus canadensis*; Veronica—*Veronica officinalis*

JULY
Plants from the side of a highway:

White clover—*Trifolium repens*; Bird's-foot trefoil—*lotus corniculatus*; Rabbit-foot clover—*Trifolium arvense*

AUGUST
Plants from a hemlock woods:

Indian pipe—*Monotropa uniflora*; Bunchberry—*Cornus canadensis*

SEPTEMBER
Plants from a pine forest:

Partridgeberry—*Mitchella repens*; Mushrooms—*Russula, Armillariella, Amanita, Hygrophorus*

OCTOBER
Plants from a sunny hilltop:

Blueberry—*Vaccinium* sp.; Pearly everlasting—*Anaphalis margaritacea*; Spirea—*Spiraea tomentosa, S. latifolia*; Chokeberry—*Aronia melanocarpa*

NOVEMBER
Plants from a hedgerow:

Bittersweet—*Celastrus*; Witch hazel—*Hamamelis*; St. John's wort—*Hypericum*; Ground-cherry—*Physalis*; Curly dock—*Rumex*; Swamp milkweed—*Asclepias*

DECEMBER
Plants from a pine forest:

Partridgeberry—*Mitchella repens*; Wintergreen—*Gaultheria procumbens*; Club moss—*Lycopodium obscurum*

About the Author

In a long career, beginning as a young newspaperman in the West, Hal Borland has celebrated the natural life and the old virtues of the land. His brief nature editorials have delighted readers of *The New York Times* for over thirty years, and his many books—among them *When the Legends Die; High, Wide and Lonesome; Hal Borland's Book of Days;* and *A Place to Begin*—have earned him the title of dean of American outdoor writers. Born in Nebraska, Mr. Borland grew up in Colorado, and for many years worked on newspapers all over the country. Today he lives in a red-shingled farmhouse in northwestern Connecticut, where he continues to bring his unique perspective to the world around him.

About the Artist

Like Hal Borland, Anne Ophelia Dowden grew up in Colorado, and it was there she began her lifelong hobby of collecting and drawing native plants and insects. For many years her hobby has been her profession, and today she is recognized as one of America's foremost botanical illustrators. Her work has been exhibited in many museums and galleries, and has been published in major magazines throughout the country. She has written and illustrated a number of award-winning books, among them *Look at a Flower, Wild Green Things in the City,* and *The Blossom on the Bough.*